Be Free, Live Creatively™

Tap into your creative skill and live the life you want!

Srebrenica Lejla

DEDICATION

To all of my Lively Creatives, those who are bold and unapologetic- keep thriving in your God given talents. Don't be afraid to think outside of the box and be innovative. The world needs more of you. Whatever your creative skill or talent, do it with the utmost excitement and expectations to positively impact the lives of others. If you are someone who feels there is *more* to life than what you are experiencing now, trust in your creative thoughts. My hope is that when you read this book, you have a refreshed and action-inspired desire to be the Lively Creative you are destined to be.

Dear Lively Creative,

First and foremost, I would like to thank you, the reader, for having interest in this body of work. For someone who, at one point in their life, did not originally have the intent to write a book, I am truly excited to share this experience with you. I wrote this book for those who are curious, eager to learn, and appreciate direct, no fluff perspectives regarding creativity. This book is dedicated to developing your own unique perspective on what creativity is and how doing so cultivates into understanding your life's purpose.

With this book, I challenge you to think creatively, live creatively, and be creative in every aspect of your life.

"

"We all influence and inspire, in various forms of art."

– Srebrenica Lejla

Before we delve into this book, I want you to keep in mind two key terms that will help shape your perspective on unique capabilities throughout each chapter. These definitions will provide a mental constant, a reminder of how we perceive these words. As we all know, words are simply tools to further the cause of an idea or thought.

So, what's the definition of creativity anyway?

According to the *New Oxford American Dictionary*, Creativity is the, "use of the imagination or original ideas."

Now what's the definition of normal?

"Recurring at uniform intervals."

I know this seems elementary, but I'm teaching y'all something here, really. Keep these terms in mind as we move throughout Chapter One.

"We get 'educated' out of creativity."
– Sir Ken Robinson

*"Creativity is an area in which younger people have a tremen-
dous advantage, since they have an endearing habit of always
questioning past wisdom and authority."*
– Bill Hewlett

CHAPTER ONE:

Don't Color Outside the Lines
(Societal Norms)

Social acceptance.

Our creativity is defined the minute we are able to comprehend the basics in life. We are taught to keep things neat, in place, and in order. I mean, life calls for structure, right? As a child we are instructed to dress, color, and write neatly. Typically we're even reprimanded or corrected if this has not been done properly. It's all a learning process. We're taught right from wrong, while also learning to understand our personalities and how they mesh with the decisions we make in life. Think about a time during your childhood in which you felt restricted, where you felt as if you were not able to fully express yourself. These limitations are often imposed very early on in childhood. We end up getting placed in these highly restrictive boxes that do not allow room to use our minds to the fullest potential. Our educational system is probably one of the most harmful contributors to our limitless thinking and creativity.

Okay now, don't get me wrong. I've attended the best schools growing up, completed a Bachelor's degree, and even went further into obtaining a graduate degree. It is highly important to obtain an education, however there are flaws I have personally experienced that shelters the mind from that limitless thinking. For parents, it is important to create an environment to allow for cultivating their child's mind beyond the mandated curriculum and encourage their creative thoughts. I realize now more than ever, that the Arts was not ever really fully supported in the school system. Many even argue that it's silly for a college student to major in any Arts. For an example, Poetry or Creative Writing. Many believe and expect that a major to be chosen in college *must* provide a direct result in to a good paying career.

Seems pretty logical to me, given the cost of education in the United States skyrocketed, even taking into consideration inflation and the changing value of the American Dollar. The question that is most often asked is, how will you get paid and make a decent living? That's the thought process that kills the desire for creative thinking, making a decent living, and being okay with living *just* above poverty level in most cases. Luckily to our evolving society, we have placed more emphasis on the individual and how each person can positively contribute to the world; in their best creative way.

For those like myself who attended private schools growing up, we had the pleasure of wearing uniforms. The use of uniforms were to ensure sameness and to reduce the occurrence of distractions with students. One could not make a big deal of someone's outfit if the entire school is wearing the same exact thing. It also provided a sense of belonging. Typically, each school would have their own color and style of uniform. If you wore a certain color, people would know to which school you belonged. Although I understand the importance of cohesion and oneness, there were many strict rules when it came to attending private schools. Your hair had to be a certain length and properly kept, (whatever the hell that means). You couldn't wear nail polish whatsoever- not even clear. I distinctly remember one time in the 8th grade I was scolded in the middle of class for wearing clear nail polish because my nails were, "too shiny." Even when it came down to the jewelry, no hoop-bangle sized earrings, not even small 'baby' hoop earrings the size of a quarter; and especially no more than one earring set at a time.

One ring was allowed on our fingers. Sounds pretty extreme for a Kindergarten through 8th grade school, right?

Others may argue that this form of discipline teaches structure and uniform, that we are all the same, we're all human. Which is true; we're all human, however there are certain things about each and every one of us that makes us stand out from the next person. We need to embrace being our true selves more. Authenticity is key. However, in society, we have taught the idea to dismiss our uniqueness and conform to a given identity that is not truly our own. Along with habits that are given to us without the sole opportunity for the individual to explore what *really* makes us who we are. Just like a child whose outlook on life is that of being limitlessly open to how they truly view themselves- without fear of judgement.

Let's take it one step further and dive deeply into how career choices are instilled into us during early development years. The most commonly asked question asked of children is,"What do you want to be when you grow up?" This simple question creates expectations that the child must become something, and usually something that will generate an acceptable income. When I was about ages 5 or 6 my teacher went around the classroom and asked that same question. I immediately shouted, "I wanna help people!"

Can you guess what happened next? Same thing that happens

when we coach our children into making proper decisions. My teacher then asked, "So you want to become a Nurse or a Doctor?" Without any second thought, I sat there, this petite chocolate child with a puff ponytail and excitement in her big brown wide eyes and replied, "Yes! I wanna be a Doctor!"

From then on, I started my interest in the Healthcare Industry. My path has led me to write this book that you are reading today. As I have gotten older and built relationships with my niece, nephews, and Goddaughter, I have shifted my way of conversing with the youth. Instead of the traditional question, I now ask, "*Who* do you want to become when you're older?" Or, "What kind of impact do you want to make in the world, with your family?" Children are full of curiosity, courage, and have an extremely impressive way of thinking. I often think about the show, *Kids Say the Darndest Things*. They truly do- their minds are that of which many adults *wish* they had when it comes to being limitless and creative. Even Michelle Obama has backed this thinking when she interviewed with Oprah Winfrey stating, "What do you want to be when you grow up is the worst question an adult can ask a kid." I wholeheartedly agree with FLOTUS.

At first, I thought these questions may come off as too complex for a child under the age of 10, however the responses I received filled me with joy. The responses included them living happy lifestyles, taking care of their future families, and helping those in need through various career choices they have been exposed to thus far in their life. I am no parenting expert, but I realize that asking children open-ended questions will foster meaningful conversations that will spark innovation and creativity. At the rate technology is moving in our world, the communication piece can become more difficult. The more freedom we have to express ourselves, the likeliness of judgment increases. Allowing someone's fears to project how you will approach a certain situation kills creative harmony and creative thinking. Society pushes us to focus solely on dollars and likes, versus what genuinely brings us happiness.

Oftentimes, our definition of normal restricts our uniqueness, the things that make us who we truly are. So many times I've heard- "Be normal, live a 'regular life,' find a good job, then retire to enjoy your hard labor." What is the real definition of a regular life? How are we teaching innovation and instilling the practice of creating a positive impact? We must remind ourselves to not turn a blind eye to our differences, but to acknowledge and embrace them. One cannot create change through being "normal." It makes you wonder if it has become that easy for us to be afraid to, 'step out of the box?' Our minds have been completely reformed and structured to think consistently with caution. We immediately compare our minds to the cause and effect of things, so much so that we place ourselves on pins and needles without even consciously realizing it. It's almost as if normality is a form of complacency. Stepping out of the status quo stretches the demand for bravery and standing out. Think about a time where intuitively you felt compelled to do something, but you were afraid because you didn't want that same feeling you had when someone told you not to color outside the lines or write neatly.

At the beginning of this chapter, you read a quote by Sir Ken Robinson, who is one of the first individuals I realized had similar views on education in schools and creativity as I. He is a New York Times Bestselling author, speaker, and advocate for encouraging the Arts in school systems throughout the world. He is also known as an expert when it comes to dissecting creativity. It is very much so true that as we grow, the less creative we can become. Luckily for some, we are able to maintain or regain that free and limitless thinking. How can we create impact if we fear boldness, uniquely being different, and being confident in our innovative ideas?

Due to those fears, our society misses out on opportunities that could be a catalyst for positive change. Imagine if Steve Jobs was afraid to color outside the lines? How would technology be different today? Think of Crayola- the most popular crayon brand. It has created such positive impact on the sole idea of creating with colors. As a result, children are excited to grab a crayon and create their own masterpieces to be displayed at school or on the refrigerator at home. Apple and Crayola encourages creativity, providing us with the tools to color outside the lines and stand out confidently.

You won't hear this often, but it's okay to think like a child. Go back to that ultra fearless, imaginative, confident, and positive child. When you are a kid, the sky's the limit. There are so many possibilities - and no one's opinion ultimately matters. Until we get older of course. We then place a high emphasis on what is or is not acceptable. And that's due to what we identify as societal norms. Our society has created this 'uniform character' that many of us feel *must* be followed. Then there are others of us who feel like rebels. That my friend is being a lively creative. Creativity causes a disturbance from disturbance. We develop things due to the lack of what is present in our lives. It creates both a negative and positive impact. Of course, you'd want your creativity and skill to leave a positive influence on the world. I have studied many creatives, successful people, infamous individuals, and those who just simply did not care whether they colored outside of the lines or not.

Time to grab your pen and journal.

How can you show up in your life and color outside the lines? The best satisfaction in life is to be true to yourself.

With the idea of 'doing right,' it is natural for us to feel one great emotion: fear. **A Lively Creative is bold, brave, and thrives in living purposefully; embracing lessons learned along the way.**

*"The thing about creativity is, people are going to laugh at it.
Get over it."*
— Twyla Tharp

*"You can't use up creativity. The more you use, the more you
have."*
— Maya Angelou

CHAPTER 2:

Fear of Failure
(Benefits of Trial & Error)

Creativity calls for trial & error. We create to express and find solution(s). We create for improvement. This very process is what brought me back to the enjoyment of creative writing. In middle school and the first couple years of high school, I wrote for personal entertainment. As I got older, I went through high school and college feeling as if I "lost" my skill of writing. I knew that this activity brought me happiness, but every time I sat down with my pen, nothing would come out. I often misinterpreted this as writer's block.

The desire to pick up exactly where I left off almost seven years ago, put me in a place of fear and void as if something important was missing from myself. I wanted to create something so bad that I clouded my mind about the actual process, rather than allowing my scattering thoughts to flow through the pen.

However, I was determined not to allow my skill to diminish so I simply started with journaling about things I'm grateful for. Put more emphasis on the things that are going well than things that are not. The fear of failure has paralyzed us so often that we completely disregard failures as lessons learned to push ourselves forward. Failure is like that nagging tug when you're going up an escalator and you get a shoestring or a piece of clothing stuck. You're distracted, embarrassed, and unmotivated to move forward because you're frustrated. Your very next thought after the incident is that you just have to be more careful and pay attention to your surroundings. Some may become so scared that you'd just avoid escalators at all costs. Awaiting perfectionism kills the opportunity for creativity. Creatives understand that projects have to be done and redone to reach the determined goal. Persistence is something often talked about, however many don't understand the discipline it takes, (we can thank social media for that). I personally anticipate the acceleration of my wonderful failures- I'll be that much closer to achieving success.

I've also spoken with so many Creatives that were on the commencement of their journeys and there is one commonality

I observed: many of them did not want to put their work out into the world because it wasn't at their level of ideal readiness. Or they've had this idea going for so long in their mind or notebook that they thought once it was out there, they'd have nothing else to produce. As a Writer, I've been there. Listen here, you have something, right now, that someone is waiting for that will change their lives for the better. It also doesn't have to be grand or extra. It could simply be your encouraging words, assisting someone to help better understand their own craft. I've been that type of person. An extreme analyst, an overachiever. I'd overlook my small victories as something I felt *everyone* already knew about or know how to do. Creatives tend to have this thing where we think everyone thinks like we do. That's the interesting perspective of the creative mind. Even to this day, I have to remind myself that some things that come *natural* to me can be a rocky mountain climb for someone else and vis a versa. This is where your magic resides.

The creative mind is also for lifelong learners. As humans we are naturally curious- we want to know what happened and how it happened. I remember when I first started taking my writing seriously, I learned to be vulnerable with myself and acknowledge my emotions. The negative emotions of fearfulness, frustration, jealousy, and even not acknowledging our distractions can hold us back. So much so to the point we don't do anything at all- that's how humans end up existing with a complacent life. Understanding the power and art of creativity is a mental healing process. The more we are in tune with ourselves, the more we are naturally inclined to live our best lives. Be open to being that lifelong learner. Your horizons are extended to create an environment for understanding life from deeper perspectives.

A Creative seeks perfectionism even when we don't realize it. We seek perfection because we fear judgment and rejection. Overthinking is the main factor of why dreams become unfulfilled. This is also when, "analysis paralysis," creeps in, and where we find ourselves stuck. I remember my father always telling me, *"Get out of the mirror."* If you stay analyzing something for too long, you'll create things to fix. We simply create those imperfections. Of course I really didn't understand this until I got older. We can look at something perfectly designed and if we over analyze, we are capable of inherently destroying a beautiful masterpiece. It is almost as if we project others perception before we enter the reality of a response. The fear of judgement and rejection is real.

Newsflash: people will judge even if 90% of the population thinks it's one of the best creations of all time. So, as the expression goes, *"Do you"*- really just go ahead and do it. Think about some of the world's greatest and successful entrepreneurs. They are the most fearless Creatives. Ironically, the most fearless Creatives are oftentimes entrepreneurs, and typically successful ones. That is a Lively Creative, being fearless. Successful entrepreneurs take action, even when things aren't quite ready. Imagine having a skill or talent that can benefit so many people, yet you decide to keep it within.

How many of you are still sitting on an idea from last year, or three years ago? Ever thought about why you haven't started? What is that *one* thing that is holding you back? If you said yourself, you've just hit the jackpot. Sometimes we get in our own way and drive ourselves into massive overthinking to the point where we take no action at all. It is perfectly okay to fail forward, and do so quickly. We cannot *not* grow or be great without the lessons learned, we call failures. However, many of us view failures as, 'signs,' that we should stop where we are. This type of thinking keeps us at square one. We must create healthy habits to minimize this way of thinking. The creative process is unique to each individual.

Understanding the very thing that motivates you to get out of bed each morning, guides you that much closer as to why you're here on this Earth. One of the habits that must be mastered is the daily practice of gratitude. Sounds simple enough. However, when it comes to creating this habit, it can be a struggle because our negative thoughts naturally inspire us. It is up to the individual to break that mold and be the identifier of what is currently good in life. The best way to start is by taking a moment to acknowledge those things, along with writing it all down.

Gratitude can open so many doors and break so many non physical barriers. Once you are in tune with yourself, the drive to be your best creative self manifests. Utilizing creativity takes courage. Whether you are an entrepreneur or in corporate America, (Yes, creativity is heavily needed in corporate settings), taking that leap to implement something different can be nerve wrecking. As discussed in Chapter One, social acceptance can be intense. Creativity is believing in your truth. That you have identified the outlet to express yourself in the most impactful way. Our society needs creative and innovative thinkers.

I often think of how James Baldwin, one of the greatest Black novelists, utilized his creative outlet of compelling words to share his story and how much of an impact he has had in literature and American society. He sparked conversations that many during his time would not be vocal about. Yet he believed in his craft and filling that personal void of what the world needed to hear, especially when it came to themes relative to the Civil Rights Movement during the 1950s-1960s.

Let's take a look into the healthcare world. Something as simple as the creative innovation of how a patient checks in for their appointment. The healthcare industry is learning to embrace innovation and improve the overall experience for the patient. Adapting to the way a traveler checks in at the airline kiosk for more efficient and faster service has changed the way many businesses approach the use of technology. Now a patient can check in for their appointment like they would check in for a flight. Creativity fills what is missing. That is how our world continues to progress towards innovation.

Creativity comes from a place of null and void. We implement things in our lives that are currently not so. We create to provide a solution. Think about the world's biggest brands and who developed them. Let's take Apple, Inc. for an example. Steve Jobs developed something so innovative, so creative, that even after so many years, people 'crave' his product. But do people really appreciate his creative process? Probably not. People care about the end product.

Why, you ask? Because the developing process for any Creative is a roller-coaster. Surprisingly there is a history of linking Creatives and Mental Health. There are the high moments of enjoying Creative Harmony, then there are also the ever so frequent moments of anxiety, the fear of our ideas not coming into fruition as we expected. As Creatives, we have this high inclination of desiring perfection. We want to first impress ourselves, others second. The fear of being misunderstood is a dangerous feeling. The frustration that leads to anxiety is that Creatives most often think that everyone else shares their exact view point. Unfortunately that is not the case. We create to share our perspective in the hopes that someone *can* relate and appreciate the creative process as well as the finished product(s).

Am I speaking to you? Okay good. Let's go a little further.

Think of a time in which you had a heightened peak of creativity. How did you feel at that particular moment? Did you immediately run to grab a pen and paper and write it down, and flush out the details later? Or did you just go at it and start your next project immediately? Creatives also have those projects that are just developed for personal use and enjoyment. For my writers out there; there are plenty of you who write and *prefer* not to share publicly because not all creative projects are meant to be shared.

That is perfectly okay because there's a huge difference between project writing and personal journaling. There are those who have that burning desire to share a part of their lives in a way that will be the pivot to bring a drastic positive change into someone's life. This is where anxiety drives us up a wall. We experience this, "Futuristic Big Picture Thinking," that oftentimes overwhelm us because there can be so many parts and pieces to this creative project we want to manifest. There are also Creatives who get lost in their creativity, manifesting the most amazing work due to the stresses of life.

Oftentimes, your pain can bring about the greatest pieces of work. Thus why the anxiety and creative process go hand in hand. Going into our creative outlets is like a stress reliever- more like a drug. The more we create, the more empowered we may feel. Anxiety fuels our creativity. Each person's creative process is different however there are two constants that never change: *creativity comes from a broken place and from the underlying desire for perfection.*

Grab that pen!

Make a list of your self-defined failures. Just relax, it does not have to be a negative experience doing this. What did you learn? How have you improved since that moment?

"Creativity takes courage."
– Henri Matisse

"Inspiration is for amateurs. The rest of us just show up and get to work."
– Chuck Close

CHAPTER 3

Feeling Inspired?
(Inspiration vs Imitation)

We create for improvement, to do what others may perceive as impossible. We also create due to the lack of things not present. The desire to manifest that transformation comes from within, and that is simply called inspiration. Inspiration drives the very existence of creativity. Inspiration causes the individual to be mentally stimulated or experience that spark of motivation to take action. It is that very same stimulation that also can confuse us when we begin to act on our momentum. Any artist, any creative, fears either imitating someone else's work, or fear of someone imitating, (or stealing for that matter), original work created by themselves. This process alone can be tricky and cause blurred lines. Even today we use the terms creatives as a label that can be so easily misused. Everyday we experience multiple moments of inspiration- things that makes us happy, freightened, and hopeful. Our environment, our circumstances inspire creativity. It's cause and effect. When we feel broken, excluded, or void, we create.

A Lively Creative naturally enjoys bringing things to life. One thing I've learned about effectively executing creativity is doing your research. Think of it as completing a homework assignment. In order to be successful, you need to do your research and check your references. As a writer, I used to be so against researching those in my niche because I didn't want to feel as if I was imitating someone else's work. I also didn't want to get distracted and get lost in thinking someone's ideas and work was better than mine. Something as simple as the name of my blog resulted in me going back to research. I had randomly picked a name for my blog when I first started. Only to realize it was already the name of a business in the same city, who had been established about five years prior. I immediately thought, *"You have GOT to be kidding me."*

Feeling extremely frustrated, I decided to research the business who was in the similar industry as me yet our messages and method were not the same. Instead of getting overly discouraged,

I continued my blog without an official name for a few months. I believed in my message and couldn't let something as simple as a lack of a blog name keep me from enhancing my skills as a Writer and Blogger. Here's what my perseverance taught me: the work I *was* doing was getting noticed and receiving positive response. I honestly could have stopped once I realized I created a blog name that was eerily similar to the business of another person. This was the exact push I needed to do *my* research in my niche of creativity and business, so that I knew how to effectively plug myself into the industry and create the impact I knew I was capable of implementing.

Once I started working with a successful business coach, I soon realized that research is what took me to the next level and that protecting intellectual property is absolutely necessary. Initially, that stage of research can be distracting because it is so easy to get caught up in what everyone else is doing. Oftentimes, we end up comparing ourselves and even lose the confidence we once had. There's no need to second guess your creative genius. It is essential to know what has been done, and what you in particular can do to add your own flavor, to spice it up. Again, humans create to fill a void. You can't fill something if you don't know the value you're capable of contributing. Let's try a visualization exercise. You go to a new restaurant, let's say a, "Build your own burrito," establishment. You have no idea how to approach the menu, although you've heard buzz that the food is pretty great. You take the bold action of, 'trying something new,' and find that although the dish was good, there are a few things you would personally add or change to your burrito. Next time you go, you make the changes based on your previous experience, thus creating a dish that is tailored to your liking. Plugging yourself into the right places allows you to blossom in your creative genius.

Now there's a blatant distinction from simply replicating someone's work and getting inspiration to launching something from your own creative realm. Don't look for inspiration. Start with what you have, what is inside you. Then do your research. What makes YOU stand out? I allow my daily circumstances to cultivate my creativity. My personal life experiences is what inspires me the most. The practice of writing out my story, my journey has allowed me to realize others have similar stories as well.

I look to fill the void. This is how I respond to such inspiration. What really inspires me is the simple idea that we all have the capability to *create the life we want*. There is no need to place our inner desires aside when we can live how we want, right now. The need to create our circumstances instead of going with the flow in life without intent makes me jump out of bed each morning, knowing I have a purpose to fulfill. I know I am achieving that as a Lively Creative, living more purposefully. Many people have reported they oftentimes feel a lack of motivation and inspiration.

The first step is to identify what organically gives you energy. What is something or someone that brings a smile to your face? A switch in your daily routine can help you see life through a brand new lens, even something as simple as taking a new route to work. To become a catalyst of change, one should be inspired and motivated to do so. Oftentimes, we think this change has to be grand and super obvious, however it does not have to be. Try a new restaurant, listen to a different type of music genre, plan a trip, or even put social media down for 24 hours. For most, the social media hiatus is a game changer. This allows you to become more present in your our own life instead of either living vicariously through someone else or shaming ourselves for not accomplishing what the next person appears to be.

Creatives have the tendency to be leery of displaying their hard work, with the fear of someone else coming to grab their ideas and manipulating them. Social media makes it so easy to seemingly replicate someone's work. Take a look at the memes that quickly spread. We enjoy someone's creative thought and application and share it all day long without the consideration of, "Hmmm, I wonder who *actually* created this meme?" Now on social media, you see that creatives place a watermark to ensure their work is being appropriately credited. I have seen so many painters whose work was reposted or even photos of individuals being used by someone else to gain followers. It can be a tough world for the genuine creatives out here. However do not become so consumed with the fear of your work being stolen that it diminishes your creative ability and most importantly, your drive.

With that being said, research is key! Learn how to properly protect your intellectual property and share your creativity with the utmost confidence, especially if you look to reap the benefits of your work.Every creative should be comfortable with putting a price tag on their work. Your intellectual property is unique to you. It should be protected simultaneously while impacting others. Those who are authentic, original, and consistent win the marathon. Think of it like baking a cake. Some people do, however in order for you to succeed in making a delicious cake, you have to see other recipes to ensure you are creating the best product. Instead of being bashful and not wanting to see how others do it, research those who *have* done it before. This allows you to add your own methods and make the recipe tailored to you. An individual cannot thrive if they do not understand their own creative process. Once that is established, the opportunities are endless.

I teach the idea that it is *not* okay to label yourself as a starving artist; you're worth much more than that. There are so many influencers and creatives on the rise that are being fearless, stepping outside the lines to determine the best alternatives that brings themselves the best creative harmony. Allowing yourself to enter into what may seem like unchartered territory can be the pivot that can change your life. Although being 'different' has become a trend, don't lose sight on being real, orignal, authentic, and consistent. People resonate with authenticity- don't go out of your way to be different. Just be you always.

Don't wait around for inspiration, create it.

Time to grab your pen and journal.

How are *you* doing things differently in your industry?

"Start where you are. Use what you have. Do what you can."
— Arthur Ashe

"Use the creative process - singing, writing, art, dance, whatever - to get to know yourself better."
— Catie Curtis

CHAPTER 4

Discover the Creator Within
(Know thyself)

Discover the Creator Within. I came across this statement one day as I was writing. This is also the same day I experienced the 'ah-ha' moment of my own creative genius through writing. It provided a fun and unique way to explore. The more I wrote, the more I discovered about myself. I even explored deeper into this through delving into home decor DIY projects and baking delicious sweet treats. However, writing is something that has been with me the longest and something I always look to improve. When you write, you are creating something, and taking an idea, and putting it on paper. You are manifesting and creating reality. That's some pretty powerful stuff. When we manifest, we are bringing something to light and understanding. We can speak life and we can write life.

Writing is a scientific occurrence. The powerful translation of our thoughts, to guide our pen across paper to bring those same things into fruition. The ability to interpret and translate our own thoughts brings great power. One of the best gifts we have is the ability to articulate and express ourselves. Whatever we think, we can become. When I started working with my very first Sales Coach, who turned into a powerful mentor, she mentioned to me that mindset is everything. Again, this goes back to scientific reality. If you're hungry, what do you typically do? You find nourishment. You communicate with your brain that an action must occur to resolve this issue. You are then convinced you must manifest results-driven actions to satisfy this need. The brain is such a powerful tool that we as humans still do not know how to fully utilize it. Crazy thing to consider, right?

We have the power to create ourselves into the individuals we are destined to be. Learning to manifest is a challenging task. Naturally, humans respond to negativity more frequently than positivity. The science behind this could be primarily due to our brain stimuli needing to protect itself from the negative things we are witnessing. It is as if we want to observe the negative things so we know what to look for in case we encounter danger. This interesting phenomenon also creates a sense of thankfulness that we, in particular, were not involved in the negative event. Next time you're scrolling through social media, think about things you are more prone to click on. Most often it is something relative to conflict and does not necessarily have a positive outcome. In our society, the majority of news outlets spew more negative news than positive. It's almost as if we've been programmed to seek negativity in the majority of our daily experiences. This can lead to constant fear and caution. It is up to us to create the positive reality.

Looking back in history and reading about those who were innovative and changed the world, you think, "How the hell did they really do it?!" I'll tell you. They, "discovered the creator within." There is no greater reward than self understanding. We cannot attempt to share our story, if we don't know who we are. When we first enter into this world, our purpose is already given to us. However, life's journey is all about how obedient we are in identifying such purpose, then acting on it. Our minds are an entire universe on their own. The things we are able to bring to life by simply believing in our own skill and talents, have always amazed me about the human mind. Earl Nightingale said it best, *"The human mind is the last great unexplored continent on Earth."*

For many of us, it takes us becoming adults, going through

many lessons learned to get back to acknowledging our Divine assignments, getting to know our true evolving selves. How does this relate to creativity you ask? The very craft of taking our own journeys to leave positive impact on someone's life in a unique way takes courage and understanding the special path in which we will take to achieve this impact. Think of it as this: before we were even born, we are assigned a specific task and life itself is a journey for us to rediscover that task and carry out our missions. You have to know yourself to be successful in all relationships: with God, our significant other, our family, and our money. Understand what you have, how much you can and are willing to give, and the manner in which you *choose* to give. One great thing I've learned, is that there is no set way or blueprint to live your truth. Being fully intune with yourself and trusting your intuition provides so much transformation to our ever evolving lives.

Here's one simple thing I've done to better connect with myself: solo dating. Not only did I learn to enjoy my own company, but I also became more in tune to what *I* enjoyed and really delve into what brings me ultimate peace. Through this, I found out that art museums are a comforting place for me. I'd go to the art museum and get lost in the details and history of art for hours. Although I do not see myself as a painter, sculptor, or art connoisseur in this form, the visuals stimulate my free creative thinking. Eventually I even graduated to bringing a journal with me to write out my reactions to certain pieces that intrigued me. This activity also provided me with new content to write about. My worldview expanded greatly.

Another for me is travel. Traveling enhances the way we interact with people, cultures, food, and most importantly, ourselves. The opportunity to take myself out of my usual routines and plug myself in new environments helps me learn how I adapt and respond to change. It's really a scientific thing. I've been able to learn what cuisine I *really* prefer, and which cities I enjoy that promotes my motivation for creativity. People often ask me to write about global travels in terms of the how-to and tips, however my best and only advice when it comes to this, is to go for it. Oftentimes, we become so cautious that we diminish the experience that was originally, deeply desired.

It's an interesting phenomenon because we dare to take the opinions of others, but fail to listen to our own. Your purpose and the method of delivery of your purpose will not be accepted nor understood by everyone. Here's why: You were placed on this Earth to impact certain people, and if you don't know who you are and what your purpose is, you are simply surviving life. Listen, I am no expert on finding purpose, however, I do know that there's a lot of inner work that must be done to reach that next level. I do understand the scientific process of creativity and how it greatly impacts our lives. Without the idea and practice of creativity, many of us would be stuck and unable to unleash our greatness. Life is ever evolving and so we should naturally do the same. Creativity is necessary for living a great quality life.

We evaluate where we are and how we can position ourselves to move forward and live our best quality of life. In 2018, I started with the mindset to mold myself into the person I'd like to be, not what people around me *wanted* me to be or what they expected me to accomplish. As I pondered this, I thought: do my actions match my thought process of how I'm actually perceived? Are my thoughts effectively manifesting to my reality? Through this, I went back to writing and practicing habits of how to be more present and aware of self. I soon realized the two didn't match up.

Can anyone else relate to this?

As I sat there, in my room writing, I thought to myself: You have the opportunity to create yourself to be any type of person you want to be perceived as. I have the capability to create opportunities for success in ALL areas of my life. Crazy right? To realize an individual could have SO much power in their own creation.

I then came up with this:

You are the controller of your destiny.

You have the power.

You OWN it.

Claim yourself as the creator.

You are only who you present yourself to be.

Sometimes we get lost and have lack of self awareness. With each new day, we have the power to write the story of how we present ourselves to the world. Create your own happiness. Create your own success. Create how you will take your failures and turn them into positive turning points in your life. Be aware of our actions towards others as well as ourselves. Some of us have goals to become more confident, more kind, more understanding, more fit, and more happy. Each day is a new opportunity to create the reality to your expectations. In 2018, I realized my niche for writing. Although I have been creatively writing since middle school, it took me years to own it and truly claim the ease of generating a compelling story. I guess you can say I gained a lot of ah-ha moments during that time. The words, "Create Yourself," kept resonating within me. We all have the ability and will power to create the person we want to be. Everyday we have a choice. Sometimes we may even catch ourselves daydreaming of the ideal life we want and the ideal person we'd like to be. It's time to remove the unconscious restrictions we place on ourselves and live in our most honest, true, form. **Once you become more intune with your ever evolving self, you'd be amazed at the growth**

and capabilities you have.

It's Journal Time!

What are some things you can do to learn yourself better?

"Do not survive life, shape it to your own will and desire"
– The Motivation Manifesto

"The most talented, thought-provoking, game-changing people are never normal."
– Richard Branson

CHAPTER 5

Time to Align
(Thoughts vs Reality)

Being the first generation college student in my immediate family, my mind was consumed with the expected success of graduating and getting a good job. Enter a career with decent pay and benefits, you know, all the good stuff. It was never instilled in me to enter a career that I personally enjoyed. Economic stability was key. Although I have been able to fall into a career in healthcare I enjoy, I knew there were other outlets for me to meet my desires to, 'help people.' One interesting thing about life is that you can have identified your purpose and fulfill the purpose, utilizing multiple avenues. You are the vessel; however you must be open and willing to *be* the vessel. I also needed to really identify how I, Srebrenica Lejla, was going to actually make that happen. There's millions of ways to help people- with some of them not having the most positive attributes. As I got older, I realized I had no idea how I would create impact in the world. Like what *really* is my purpose?

It's easy to have thoughts on what kind of person we'd like to be or what kind of lifestyle we'd like. Making the connection between our thoughts and making that connection with reality requires great vulnerability with ourselves. A Lively Creative takes the bold action to give the connection a try until it is appropriately aligned- our thoughts and our reality becoming one. When I think of creativity and developing *who* you want to become, I immediately think of some of the world's greatest scientists. They allowed their creative and futuristic thinking to uncover things that have greatly impacted the human race. Again, we create from brokeness or lack.

No matter the path we choose for ourselves, we must allow our creative thought process to flourish and openly be a part of our lives. Even things as simple as how you'd like to style your hair or what you'd like to wear, utilizes creativity. Commonly, there are many of us who'd like to be the individual that can be creative and wear colorful and diverse hairstyles, however in reality there's a mental box that is developed and the thought of the hairstyle is simply just that- a thought. It is that same mental block that prevents many from living and leading the life of genuine wholeness and happiness.

I remember having a conversation with a group of friends and someone mentioned, *"Why wait to live when you're retired? So many retired people have not uncovered their passion or purpose that they spend a whole life unfulfilled."* As I sat there to let the thought resonate, I realized how powerful that statement was. How many individuals you know are retired and 'bored' with life? It seems that we live to check things off our goals list, then what? Utilizing your creative abilities and skill leads to uncovering life's purpose. It's bewildering that so many people may never get a chance to uncover their purpose or gift. Stepping into your gift requires a lot of change- for the better of course. However being confident in yourself provides the best transformation. It is truly priceless.

I distinctly remember breaking out of my quiet, timid, shell in high school. I was the one who didn't say much because I didn't want my opinions or decisions to make a disturbance. I just went with the flow of the desires of others. It wasn't until I became an adult and really delved into my own being, that I soon realized the fun, goofy, witty, and outgoing person within was not being displayed outwardly. Ever have thoughts of who you *truly* are, but unsure of how to actually express that? Many of us have experienced the struggle of doing what we enjoy versus dealing with our reality. I mean, how hard could it be, right? Align your inner world with your outer world and boom, you're all set! The reality is, this process can be tough because it connects the mental, physical and spiritual being into one. For many of us that process takes much preparation. One may consider doing a career change and have the end result of living the desired life because of that change. This may all be played out internally, however our day-to-day actions show no sense of expecting that into fruition. Ultimately, the results end in the romanticization of the inner desires that may never be brought to life.

Think about the virtual reality headsets. We get to choose the experience we want to have during our virtual ride, living vicariously through a preprogrammed screen. In those very same moments, the outer world, the *real* reality, is completely discarded. While we have the virtual headsets on, our main concern is that while we're going for the ride, as long as our physical bodies are stationary, complacent, and safe, we can enjoy the virtual ride as long as we desire. This is very much how the lack of alignment works in life. The ease of drifting off into a mental or virtual reality to create and experience things that may not be readily available in the real world can place an individual in a dangerous place when it comes to life's alignment with purpose. It's time we get out of our own heads and utilize the skills we have to create the reality *we* want for ourselves.

Cultivating creativity requires one to not overthink. Too often it is expected that everything has to be perfectly aligned, from our viewpoint, in order to allow things to flourish. We cannot allow the fears of others to project how our realities are created. If you feel like you want to try that new lipstick, do it- why *not*? If you're one of the young fellas with the locs and dreads and want to try something new by cutting your hair? Do it- *why not*? It's amazing how often we could put our own desires aside just to please others. Even for myself, through many trials and error, I had to learn that my view and perspective on what is best aligned for my life is all that matters. Once we are truly in tune with ourselves we harvest a natural flow of thinking. The freedom you are looking to achieve in life requires you to be free within yourself. In that journey of being free within, Creatives constantly seek information to calculate the next step. Alignment requires bridging the gap. In order to do so, each individual must be able to incorporate free thinking in a way that creativity can be nurtured and be active. **It's time to align the person you want to be with the person that you are.**

It's journal time!

Think about your dream job as a child. How has that evolved into your adulthood?

"Harmony makes small things grow, lack of it makes great things decay."
– Sallust

"The way of the Creative works through change and transformation, so that each thing receives its true nature and destiny and comes into permanent accord with the Great Harmony: this is what furthers and what perseveres."
– Alexander Pope

CHAPTER 6

It's All About Harmony

Harmony. This is where many individuals get stuck-understanding their unique creative process. Although in reality it's not much to it. Once you are intune with yourself, everything else will follow. There are three simple steps to achieve this: know what you want, identify your space to work, and allot time for execution. Even with this simple formula, many still struggle with obtaining a natural creative flow. Here's the breakdown:

Know what you want: Identifying what *you* want versus the expectations of others is life- changing.

– Take the necessary time to date yourself, even if it's cooking your favorite dish or exploring a new movie genre. Be *okay* with moments of planned solidarity.

– Journal. Even if you aren't a, "writer," don't let that stop you from putting pen to paper and expressing your thoughts.

– Get a bit more creative- create personal voice memos or even videos to visualize how you are presented to the world. This is also very fun.

Determine your Creative Space

Whether you are a Writer, a Painter, or want to explore your creative side, having a designated space to work is essential. Curating your personal creative space not only enhances creativity, but also you'll learn more about yourself. The physical, mental, and emotional benefits will inspire you to create your very own space right away. Allow your creativity to flourish and watch your artistic side explode. Here are lucrative steps for a creative working space.

Step 1: Don't overthink the size and style of your space. Your space can be as simple as a small corner in the room that has all of your favorite things. It's not necessary to have a gigantic office space- especially if you're just starting out with curating your first dedicated space for creativity. It is perfectly okay to start small.

Step 2: Identify objects and colors that naturally appeal to you. For me, I started off with falling in love with pineapples, the color yellow, and random artwork that I'd either painted or purchased. I'm a writer, so cute journals and some of my favorite books are nicely stacked on my makeshift desk.

Step 3: Bring some LIFE to your area! Natural lighting, if possible is great for any creative that is in need of motivation and inspiration. If you can't get that natural lighting just right, consider getting a nice aesthetic lamp. For my personal space, I chose natural lighting and smell good candles. Good scents set the mood for me. Another is adding a plant to your space. Having another source of life in the room such as a plant can be mentally stimulating.

Step 4: Put some love in your creative space! Only you can love your space and feel the most comfortable. Think of it as a method of self care. Nurturing your creative thoughts alleviates anxiety and aids with managing depression, (I am not a clinician, or Doctor). Be proud of the work you produce.

Step 5: Be open to evolving your creativity. It's important to be open minded with your creative skill and ability. Don't just fixate yourself to one thing i.e., writing. Explore various outlets so that you can learn more about you.

Allot time for Execution

We all have a passion or even something we just simply enjoy as a hobby. The number one excuse we give ourselves for not experiencing them is time. The anticipation of, "getting around to it," is mentally instilled in our minds, but the time never comes. As a result, many of us feel like time is quickly passing by and find ourselves stuck, in a vicious cycle of thinking versus doing. We can get so caught up in our daily routines that we no longer become present in our own lives. Here are seven lucrative steps for increasing time management in a busy world. As with any habit, it takes commitment and consistency:

1. Write a weekly priority list.
2. Find the times of the day/week you are most productive.
3. Identify your distractions, work to minimize them.
4. Break large tasks into smaller tasks.
5. Execute your action plan.
6. Evaluate *your* process.
7. Repeat until you've created a lucrative system that works for *you*

Your Action Items

− Grab a calendar or notebook, (or both!)

− Document your current daily schedule, (just one day). The time you get up, work, gym, how often you check your e-mail/social media, time with family, gym and cooking.

− Choose one thing you'd like to work on for the next seven days. Whether it is reading for 30 minutes, going to the gym 3-4 times in one week, watch less tv, or go on a social media hiatus.

− Each day, document your activities and goals accomplished.

− Through creating a daily task list, the human mind receives signals for us to feel gratification and accomplishment once we check off an item on our list. This keeps us inspired and motivated to further achieve our goals.

For many of us Creatives, especially writers, there are three key steps to achieve creative harmony in written work: Read. Write. Repeat.

To be a writer, you must first be a reader. Understanding the essentials is key. You will be able to determine your preferred writing style and genres you are attracted to. Like any artist, you must be inspired. Read, write, and repeat. When in doubt, read. Explore various topics, and broaden your experiences through this avenue. Find an interesting book or article. Read then write about your reaction or response. Or, if the reading, "sparks," something within you, write.

As a writer, we are our own strongest critics. ***Writing requires creating a habit.***

Think about it like this: you want to become a bodybuilder. However there are repetitive steps and proper habits to form in order to become competitive. Let's say you want to become a great baker. Same formation. Create proper habits. Whatever your goals are. Start with writing how you feel at the moment. Reflect on your day. For those who want to creatively write, create a list of the themes and topics that attract you. Words that inspire. I call this, "free writing." Free writing allows room for all creative content. Creating on a blank canvas may sound scary and intimidating, however we all must start with something. I challenge you so that you may begin your journey of finding your true and authentic voice.

The results of achieving creative harmony are that people are typically more happy and more confident in their work. **The more you work on your craft, the more you are able to see yourself as the expert.**

You guessed right, it's pen time!

What is one thing you can implement into your schedule to initiate harmony in your life?

"Create your own visual style... let it be unique for yourself and yet identifiable for others."
– Orson Welles

"The role of a creative leader is not to have all the ideas; it's to create a culture where everyone can have ideas and feel that they're valued."
– Ken Robinson

CHAPTER 7

Be Free, Live Creatively

I wrote this book so that your perception of creativity and influence is elevated and you take a new lens on your purpose in life. Some of us have heard the concept of, "Thrive in life, not simply survive life." There is no singular definition to success, for success is determined by the individual. I was only able to define what success meant to me when I delved into things that interested me. I learned what I genuinely liked, things I didn't care for, and truly understanding what I want. It becomes difficult to ask for things that you don't know the reason as to *why* you want those things. Many desire more money. But why? What is the real underlying factor that will bring you to your state of peace? Others want to travel more. Have you really sat down and thought about *why* this desire is so strong for you?

Be Free, Live Creatively is something that I have subconsciously worked on for the last four years. Taking my experiences, observations from my childhood, and implicating practices of understanding that my life and my purpose is much bigger than myself. Many of us go through life not understanding *why* we're here and *how* we should be living out our purpose. It's simple. Follow your intuition, believe in yourself, and take action. You can't create positive impact living on fear and safety of things being fine the way they are. You think if Steve Jobs, the creator of Apple, Inc., would have allowed perfectionism, the fear of doing something that has never been done, and staying persistent in his vision that we would have one of the world's leading products in technology.

Creativity *is* aligned with purpose. Our methods to live out our purpose evolves, so does our limitless creativity. Life can be a funny thing sometimes. It all drives back to our intuition. Some of us are in tune with our intuition while others seem to wander around the same patterns because we haven't learned to quiet our spirit to be led and guided for success. This book was written to challenge your thought process. How can you effectively show up in your life daily to express your creative thoughts? Do we choose to fail forward or do we become complacent with getting by in life because that feels like the safest thing to do. If nothing else, do what genuinely brings you joy. Everything else will fall into place and naturally you will create positive impact. Elevating yourself can be a tough road and the process of evolving can be a painfully beautiful process. No matter where you are, what you do, start each day with the mindset to be great. No one has to believe in you or your mission right now. Keep pushing anyway. If this is you allow this time to increase your skill and expand your knowledge.

I know the typical saying is not to think like a child- however, I want you to go back into your childhood. Think about those moments that you were so hopeful that nothing could make you feel otherwise. Go back to when you were curious, you were that information and detail seeker. Think about how your mind was a playing field for endless imagination and possibility. Life is an ongoing process and we will forever learn more and more of ourselves. Oh the things achieved when the mind is limitless! As Earl Nightingale states, *"The human mind is the last, great unexplored continent on the Earth."* It is truly amazing the things we are capable of, if we put our minds to it.

I also want you to think about this. When was a time you felt your idea or dream was crushed as a child. You confided in someone of your huge dream, but they immediately shut you down. How did that feel? Do you still think they are right today? How do you think that has affected your desires for success from that moment forward? Do you feel you've overcome the naysayers? The best revenge is success, whatever you measure success by.

We are all influencers. We have impact over at least one other individual in the world, whether we know it or not. Creativity cannot be destroyed. Creativity is within you. It can be lost. It *has* been lost. It's like finding your purpose in life. You keep going until you have a revelation. Then you take action. Taking action is essential. This is where most of us get lost in transition. The action part.

As we grow older, our creativity diminishes. We're taught to, 'think more realistically,' and be our own, "Debbie Downers." Kinda sick, right? To think we sabotage ourselves mentally so easily? This is all from learned behavior. Our definition of success is given to us very early on in our lives. Art is consistently viewed as a 'starving artist' realm and there's no gold at the end of the rainbow for us. We conform to the majority and trends of society, then wonder why we are lost, stuck, and even unhappy in our lives? The instilled fear creates this relentless idea of daring not to do something 'crazy' which is all creativity. Don't allow someone's fear of creativity and growth to diminish your ability to pivot your life to the next level. For the millennials out there- those who are daring to go against the status quo, it is important to keep in mind our past, so we can improve our future. Each individual can groom themselves to be a catalyst for positive impact and change. However, don't be afraid to push boundaries. Remember to be okay with coloring outside the lines. What we identify as mistakes or failures are simply experienced for the greater good of our evolvement. I used to think I couldn't be successful until I failed miserably at everything - I would start projects with the anticipation to struggle so that I can 'earn' my right to success. It took me continuously taking action and being bold to realize you *don't* have to suffer and struggle to achieve success and happiness. Everyone's story and path is unique. Allow yourself to try new things or really start paying attention to the things that bring you peace. From there, permit yourself to evolve and keep an open mind for necessary growth. The need to be free within ourselves is not only necessary, it is an absolute requirement.

Thanks for coming along for the ride.

Here's your final pen thought:

What does being free, and living creatively look like to you?

"Be Bold, Be Confident, Be You! Be a Lively Creative."
– Srebrenica Lejla

The Lively Creative Manifesto

A Lively Creative is a doer, a go-getter who unapologetically believes in their ability to be ah-mazing. Not only do we seamlessly create, we expand barriers and provoke thoughts of the human mind. We are not tied to one avenue of creativity- we are multifaceted. The Lively Creative's mind is that of an individual who embraces growth and development, even the moments that are not so glamorous. We are not shy in our efforts, but display our works with the most humble, yet undeniable confidence in the art we produce. We are open to various walks of life to enhance our worldview. We do not wait for opportunity, we create it. Our brokenness does not define us, yet it is a catalyst to impose positive impact on the world through our experiences. We do not take it lightly that others may look at us in awe of the harmony of our creative genius, leaving them wondering how could we have crafted something so beautiful.

Be Free, Live Creatively™

ABOUT THE AUTHOR

Srebrenica Lejla is a Copywriter & Strategist for emerging entrepreneurs, Lifestyle Blogger, and Creative Mentor. Teaching others to *Discover the Creator Within*, individuals are able to place themselves on authentic platforms for their stories to be heard. Starting with her own victories of writing and pitching to publications with large followings, Lejla knew there were others who desired the same. In her supportive Facebook Group, The Lively Creatives, individuals are able to share their art, successes and struggles with creating and sharing their work with one another. She has also had success with implementing The Creative's VMA Course, which walks writers through the process of visualizing, monetizing, and actualizing their goals as writers. Through this, people in her community are able to reap the benefits of powerful collaborations, for she believes there is much power in unity. Her first published book has been derived from her Lifestyle Blog, www.thelivelycreative.com, focusing on mental health, life inspiration, and some of her crafty projects.

Srebrenica Lejla also specifically helps business owners convey their brands to provide magnetic messaging that converts into profits. Many business are sitting on gold mines and just magical words to connect with their people. Lejla also provides group and one on one coaching to help writers understand their creative process and create effective time management for their writing. You may even catch her written work in *The Queen Boss Rise Anthology*, sharing her experiences and lessons learned as an emerging entrepreneur. Just from taking the courage to get back in the habit of putting pen to paper, Lejla has excelled by becoming a two-time author in less than a year. As an MBA candidate, Srebrenica Lejla also enjoys crafty DIY projects, baking sweet treats, and exploring around the world.

You can learn more about Srebrenica Lejla via:
Email: sb@thelivelycreative.com
www.thelivelycreative.com
FB/IG: @srebrenicalejla

Made in the USA
Lexington, KY
07 November 2019